NICOLÒ SUFF

ST. PETER'S

GUIDE
TO THE SQUARE
AND
THE BASILICA

LIBRERIA EDITRICE VATICANA
00120 CITTÀ DEL VATICANO

Contents

Translated by Kate Marcelin-Rice

Photos: Archivio Tipografia Vaticana, G. Galazka,
F. Marzi, G. Pera (Elle Di Ci), Del Priore.

© Copyright 1998 - Libreria Editrice Vaticana - Città del Vaticano
Tel. (06) 698.85003 - Fax (06) 698.84716

ISBN 88-209-2480-3

Tipografia Vaticana 1999

Peter's authority in the group of the Apostles

One day, during a journey to the source of the River Jordan at the foot of the imposing Mount Hermon range in Northern Palestine, Jesus made a solemn promise to Simon, son of John "You are 'Rock ', and on this rock I will build my Church, and the jaws of death shall not prevail against it" (Mt 16:18). With these words Jesus changed Simon's name to Peter, desiring in this way to make all those present understand that he was about to trust Simon Peter with an important task: to be the foundation stone of his Church. Since the word "Church" means "assembly", that is, a "gathering" of people, at that moment Jesus was predicting that Peter would be the basis of the assembly he would gather.

In fact, Jesus came down to earth to gather around him men who were straying like sheep without a shepherd. As a "good shepherd", he wanted to found his Church for them. But he met with ferocious opposition, so that he was condemned to death and hung on a cross. Then the flock he had started to gather were once again in grave danger of being scattered. However, precisely to avert this risk, during the Last Supper and his agony in the garden on the Mount of Olives, Jesus prayed ardently to his Father. And his prayers were heard. Jesus "was raised" and, after his resurrection, he made certain that his own institution would endure by telling Peter: "Tend my sheep" (Jn 21:16). In other words, "Peter, take my place as shepherd". At that very moment Jesus, the only true shepherd of those who believe in him, gave Peter his task and so kept the promise he had made a few months earlier.

Indeed, after Jesus had ascended into heaven, Peter acted as leader of the Apostles, taking Jesus' place. In fact, the Book of the Acts of the Apostles tells us that after the ascension of Jesus, it was Peter who, by choosing Matthias, took the initiative of completing the College of the Apostles which had lost one member due to Judas' betrayal. Again, it was Peter, on behalf of all the others, who preached to the Jews of Jerusalem and spoke before the council. It was Peter who condemned profiteers, such as Ananaias and Sapphira. It was Peter who opened the Church to pagans by baptizing Cornelius, the Roman centurion. It was Peter who spoke decisively and conclusively before the Sanhedrin, gathered in Jerusalem.

In brief, the Gospel and the Acts of the Apostles tell us that during his lifetime Peter exercised indisputable authority in the group of the Apostles. Catholic Christians, taking as their basis these passages from the Gospel and the Acts of the Apostles, believe that Peter's authority has been passed on to his successors, the popes. This is why they claim that the Pope, Successor of Peter, is Christ's Vicar on earth.

Peter, first Bishop of Rome

The Acts of the Apostles tell us that after Jesus' death and resurrection, Peter stayed on in Jerusalem for a while. Then when the Jewish persecution of the Christians broke out, he fled "to another place". From this moment the Acts say nothing further about Peter, but from other sources we know that he lived for some time in Antioch, Syria, and then went to Rome, the capital of the Roman Empire which was spreading throughout the known world. In Rome, Peter suffered martyrdom.

That Peter came to Rome and was martyred there is confirmed by an impressive mass of writings which date to apostolic times. There is already a reference to this in the first of the two Letters written by Peter himself, as well as in Paul's Letter to the Romans. A little later, Clement, a Bishop of Rome, in a letter written in about 95, stated that Peter had been martyred in Rome. Papias, the elderly Bishop of Hierapolis who knew several of the Apostles' disciples, says that Peter preached in Rome. In about the year 180, Irenaeus, Bishop of Lyons in France and Dionysius, Bishop of Corinth in Greece, told of Peter's time in Rome in their writings. This mass of documentation has been confirmed by recent excavations under St. Peter's Basilica, which have brought to light many stone tablets and inscriptions which show that Peter's memory was already venerated on the Vatican Hill by about 120. These sources confirm what the Roman priest, Gaius, who lived in the second century, had said in his response to an enemy of the Christians: "Go to the place called Vatican or on the road to Ostia: there you will find the trophies of the founders of the Church of Rome" (in

The Chair of Peter. The imperial throne of Charles the Bald, presented to the Pope in 870.

other words, the tombs of Peter and Paul). Gregory of Tours, the French Bishop, also wrote: "Peter's tomb is located beneath the altar of the basilica built by Constantine".

Peter's martyrdom in Rome

The historian Tacitus relates that during the night of July 19 in 64 AD an enormous fire started at the foot of the Palatine Hill, and the blaze destroyed whole quarters of the city. The crowds, who knew that Nero wanted to build a more beautiful Rome, immediately suspected that it was he who had given orders to set fire to the town. A sullen discontent spread so rapidly among the people that Nero took fright. To defend himself from the accusation of having started the fire, he blamed the Christians and unleashed a furious persecution against them.

Caligula's Circus on the Vatican Hill

On the other side of the Tiber at the foot of the Vatican Hill, Nero possessed a magnificent circus, the Circus of Caligula, commonly known as Nero's Circus. In the center stood the obelisk which the Emperor Caligula had had brought from Heliopolis in Egypt. In this circus the Roman people could watch the spectacle of the punishments inflicted by the Emperor on those who were supposed to have started the fire. Here too, many Christians were flung as food to wild beasts; others were nailed to planks in the form of a cross; and yet others, sprinkled with pitch, resin and sulphur, acted as live torches to illuminate the games that lasted all night long in the Emperor's gardens.

The bodies of these Christian martyrs were interred on the neighboring slopes of the Vatican Hill, where a burial ground already existed.

The recent excavations, which began in 1940 and were opened to the public for the first time in the Holy Year 1950, have demonstrated that at the end of the first century AD and during the second century, this zone had become a sepul-chral area which was therefore pro-tected by Roman law, and that the subsoil beneath the Vatican Hill is still a maze of ancient tombs today. During the excavations, archaeologists noted that all the tombs converge toward one specific tomb and that in about 160 (it was possible to establish this date because on the bricks several seals from the period of Marcus Aurelius have been identified) a brick wall was built, covered in plaster of a reddish color, which curves around that particularly venerated tomb, forming a niche. In this niche, above the tomb covered with a marble slab, were two small columns. They supported another slab, of travertine, in the form of a table, which divided the niche into two super-imposed "aedi-cole". During the third century, a new section of wall was built perpendicular to the "red wall", known as "wall G" because of the graffitti scratched on it by the unknown hands of visitors who came to pray at this venerated tomb. Experts have been able to identify the letters of one graffito on the "red wall" as: PETR, the first letters of the Greek name

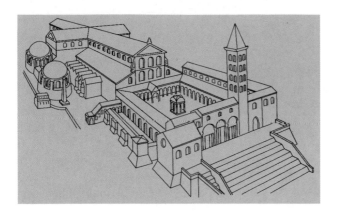

Elevation of the Constantinian Basilica

Petros, Peter; and EN, which, with the addition of the letter "i", now obliterated, form "eni", that is, "is here"; "Peter is here". It was therefore possible to deduce that this "aedicola" is the same "tropaion" which Eusebius mentioned, that is, the victory monument which preserves the memorial of Peter whose "trophy" was mentioned by the priest Gaius in about 200. To conclude, archaeological excavations have made it possible to identify the precise place where Peter is buried, beneath the present altar of the "Confessio".

The Constantinian Basilica of St. Peter's

In 313 the Emperor Constantine (306-337), who had become lord of the Roman Empire, granted the Christians full freedom. Then to win their friendship, he decided to build a basilica over St. Peter's tomb. To make room for it, he cut into the Vatican hill and covered many of the tombs. He then had a broad foundation wall built and in 324 the construction of a majestic basilica began. It was consecrated in 326 by Pope St. Silvester and completed in about 349 by Constantius, Constantine's son. In this basilica, Peter's tomb, closed on three sides, was open toward the East and the faithful could see it until the time of Pope Gregory the Great (590-604), when the pavement was raised and an altar built over the tomb, over which another was later built by Callistus II (1119-1124).

In front of Constantine's basilica was an imposing four-porticoed courtyard, reached by climbing a flight of 35 steps. It was entered through five doors leading to five aisles, bordered by four rows of 22 columns each. The basilica was paved in marble of various colors and had a wooden ceiling.

Down the centuries the basilica's walls were adorned with mosaics, pictures and statues. Many artists worked on them, including Giotto, Perugino, Donatello, Filarete, Pollaiolo, but almost all their works have gone astray. Various alterations were also made and certain features added, in order to build tombs for the emperors and popes who wished to be buried near Peter's tomb.

For 12 centuries the Constantinian basilica was the center of worship and the destination of pilgrimages for Christians who came to Rome from all over the world to "see Peter", and so to strengthen their faith.

The nave of the Constantinian Basilica, from a fresco by Domenico Tasselli

The new St. Peter's Basilica

However, the splendid basilica was repeatedly sacked during barbarian invasions, and during the period of the popes' exile in Avignon it fell into disrepair. It was frequently reinforced and restored, but toward the middle of the 15th century it became obvious that henceforth no restoration would suffice. Atmospheric factors, the barbarian invasions, wars, sacking and neglect during the Avignon period had reduced the basilica's structural walls to such a precarious state that it threatened to collapse. Pope Nicholas V (1447-1455) therefore felt the time had come to

St. Peter's, after a drawing by Maarten van Heemskerck, c. 1523

rebuild it completely. He commissioned Leon Battista Alberti to draft the plan for a new basilica and entrusted the direction of the work to Bernardo Rossellino. However he had hardly started when the Pope died. Under his successors, Pius II, Paul II, Sixtus IV and Alexander VI, the work continued, albeit at a very slow pace.

It took a decisive turn with the election of Pope Julius II (1503-1513). He made the brave decision to begin demolishing part of the old basilica and to resume the project interrupted by the death of Nicholas V. The architect Donato Bramante was put in charge of the new basilica's construction. He set to work immediately, preparing new plans and beginning to pull down the old walls, starting with the central section. Chroniclers of the time say that the demolition of the walls was a fascinating and tremendous spectacle.

On April 18, 1506, the Pope laid the foundation stone of the new basilica.

Commemorative stone tablet on the basilica's façade (Pius VII, 1780)

Donato Bramante, who had planned a basilica in the form of a Greek cross, immediately began to excavate and built the four great structural piers destined to support the weight of the dome, thereby determining the future basilica's basic structure. With the death of Julius II in 1513 and that of Bramante the following year, work was interrupted. It then continued with alternating events and frequent changes of design under the following pontiffs: Leo X (1513-1521), Clement VII (1523-1534), Paul III (1534-1549), Julius III (1550-1555), Paul IV (1555-1559), Pius IV (1559-1565), Pius V (1566-1572), Gregory XIII (1572-1585), Sixtus V (1585-1590), Clement VIII (1592-1605), Paul V (1605-1621). These popes entrusted the planning and direction of the work site to various architects: Raphael (Sanzio) from 1514 to 1520, aided by Giuliano da Sangallo and Fra Giocondo da Verona, Antonio da Sangallo the Elder from 1520, Baldassare Peruzzi from 1538, Antonio da Sangallo the Younger and Michelangelo Buonarrotti from 1546 to 1564, Pirro Ligorio, Jacopo Barozzi, known as Vignola, who died in 1572, Giacomo della Porta from 1572, Domenico Fontana, Carlo Maderno, who was responsible for the façade and, from 1629, Gian Lorenzo Bernini, who gave the interior its present aspect.

Michelangelo took on the direction of the work when he was already 72 years old but gave it a great impetus, working on it for 16 years. In 1557, when the need arose to decide on the type of roof the basilica required and so on how to raise the dome, it was he who had a wooden model of it built; this took him three years, and he started the con-

struction work but was unable to finish it. By the time he died in 1564, work on the dome had reached the level of the drum and he had constructed the areas for the four corner chapels: the Gregorian chapel, the Chapel of St. Michael Archangel and St. Petronilla, the Clementine Chapel and the Chapel of Our Lady of the Column.

The architects who succeeded him carried on building various parts of the basilica but constantly postponed the construction of the dome, until in 1587 Sixtus V decided to commission Giacomo Della Porta to complete it. He took two years to do so, finishing it on May 21, 1590.

Nonetheless it was not given the final touch until June 1593 when the lantern was built and the cross set on its summit, about 136 m. high.

The forepart of the Constantinian basilica with its portico and façade was still standing. In 1607, Paul V announced a competition for the construction of the façade. Carlo Maderno (1556-1629) won and built it between 1608 and 1612, partly modifying the plans left by Michelangelo.

The pediment of the façade bears the name of Paul V and the date 1612. In the meantime, Maderno had the relics and funeral monuments from the ancient basilica moved to the Vatican Grottoes and in the resulting space extended the three aisles, giving the basilica its present form of a Latin cross and adding three new side chapels.

After Maderno, Urban VIII (1623-1644) put Gian Lorenzo Bernini (1598-1680) in charge, and at last, on November 18, 1626, 1,300 years after the consecration of the first basilica, the Pope was able to solemnly consecrate the new one.

After Bernini, Innocent XI (1676-1689) appointed Carlo Fontana (1634-1714) to direct the work.

St. Peter's Square

Once the basilica had been built, it was felt that a space should be created in front of it with a capacity sufficient to contain the mass of people who would flock here to take part in the most solemn functions, especially on the occasion of the celebrations for the Feast of Corpus Christi which was then very popular and widely observed. It was Pope Alexander VII (1655-1667) who decided to build the square as we know it today—it had actually already been begun by Sixtus V when he had the obelisk moved there—and it was continued by various popes. In 1656, Alexander VII entrusted the direction of the work to Gian Lorenzo Bernini who completed it very rapidly, between 1657 and 1667.

St. Peter's Square has the shape of an immense ellipse (the visitor who stands in one of the two centers of this ellipse, marked by two white disks, one on each side of the obelisk, sees a single row of columns), 320 m. long and 240 m. wide, at its broadest point.

The square is bordered by a *double colonnade* with 284 Doric columns and 88 pilasters of travertine marble. These columns, 13 m. tall, are arranged in four rows and give the colonnade a breadth of 17 m. The superimposed trabeation surmounted by a balustrade gives it an overall height of 21 m.

Bernini built two straight covered wings (galleries) 120 m. long, to link the two wings which, with the basilica's façade, give the colonnade its oval form. The wing on the left is the Charlemagne Wing. At the top end, level with the square, various services are provided: the washrooms, the Information Office, the first aid room, the Vatican Post Offices, the book shop *Libreria Editrice Vaticana,* and rooms for the guard.

Charlemagne Wing,
on the left of the square

Between the Charlemagne Wing and the basilica's façade is the *Campano* Arch, one of the entrances to the Vatican. Starting from this point, between the pilaster strips of the façade are the stations of the Cross in bronze which continue along the Constantine Wing on the right.

Where the *Constantine Wing* begins, under the colonnade is the "Bronze Door" through which, ascending the "Scala Regia" (royal stairway), the Vatican Palace is reached. Standing on the colonnade and on the two straight wings are *140 statues,* 3 m. tall, and the large heraldic emblems of Alexander VII who commissioned Bernini to make them.

The statues on the southern side (to the left) represent the following saints: above the colonnade: Norbert; Thibaut; Theodore, martyr; Jerome; Hilarion; Bruno; Louis Bertrand; John the Almsgiver; Romuald; Joseph, husband of Mary; Peter Nolasco; Paul the Hermit; Anthony Abbot; Francis de Paola; Anthony of Padua; Charles Borromeo; Philip Neri; Philip Benizi; Cajetan; Fran-

Bronze door, leading to the Constantine Wing

Some of the 140 statues of saints adorning the balustrade of the two semicircular arms of the square

cis Xavier; Hyacinth; Theodora, virgin and martyr; Beatrice, virgin; Rose of Lima; Galla, the Widow; Marcellinus, pope and martyr; Sylvester, pope; Martin, pope and martyr; Marcellus, pope and martyr; Peter Celestine, pope; Clement, pope and martyr; Leo IV, pope; Gregory of Nazanzius; Ubaldo, bishop; John Chrysostom; Athanasius, bishop; Leo the Great, pope; Alexander, bishop; Ignatius, bishop and martyr; Spyridon, bishop; Eusebius, bishop; Romanus, martyr; Stephen, martyr; Laurence, martyr; on the Charlemagne Wing: Denys, martyr; Pancratius, martyr; Pelagia; Crescentius, martyr; Andrew Corsini; Constance, martyr; Felix, martyr; Achilleus, martyr; Nereus, martyr; Julian, martyr; Paul, Martyr; Basiledes, martyr; Hyppolitus, martyr; Felician, martyr; Sebastian, martyr; Fabian, Pope; Pudentiana, virgin; Praxedes, virgin; Modestus, martyr; Vitus, martyr; Marcellinus, martyr; Mark, martyr, and Bonadventure.

The statues above the northern wing (on the right) represent the following saints: on the colonnade: Gallicanus, martyr; Leonard; Petronilla, virgin; Vitalis, martyr; Techla, virgin and martyr; Albert the Carmelite; Elizabeth, queen; Agatha, virgin and martyr; Ursula, virgin and martyr; Clare, virgin; Olympia, widow; Lucy, virgin and martyr; Balbina, virgin and martyr; Apollonia, virgin and martyr; Remigius, bishop; Ignatius of Loyola; Benedict; Bernard; Francis of Assisi; Dominic; John Damascene; Theodosia, virgin and martyr; Polycarp, bishop and martyr; Mary of Egypt; Mark the Evangelist; Febronia, virgin and martyr; Fabiola, widow; Nilamon the Lonely; Marcianus, martyr; Eusignius, martyr; Marinus, martyr; Dydimius, martyr; Apollonius, martyr; Candida, virgin and martyr; Fausta, martyr; Barbara, virgin and martyr; Benignus, martyr; Malco, martyr; Marmant, martyr; Columba, virgin and martyr; Pontian, pope and martyr; Genesius, martyr; Agnes, virgin and martyr; Catherine, virgin and martyr; on the Constantine Wing: Justin, martyr; Cecilia, virgin and martyr; Frances of Rome; George, martyr; Magdalen de' Pazzi; Susanna, virgin and martyr; Martina, virgin and martyr; Nicholas of Bari; Nicholas of Tolentino; Francis Borgia; Francis de Sales; Theresa, virgin; Juliana, virgin and martyr; Julian, Bishop; Celsius, martyr; Anastasius, martyr; Vincent, martyr, Paul, martyr; John, martyr; Damian, martyr; Cosima, martyr; Zosimus, martyr; Rufus, martyr; Protase, martyr; Gervase, martyr, and Thomas Aquinas.

Pilgrims arriving to visit St. Peter's have the impression they are welcomed by the two immense arms of the colonnade which embrace the square, an image of the Church welcoming all her faithful. The Christian people gathered there, noticing the statues set on the colonnade, feel they are invited to look ahead to the heavenly Church.

Always open to the public, the square affords the visitor a continuous opportunity to meet pilgrims from all over the world who have come to pray at St. Peter's tomb and to see and hear the Pope and pray with him. Every Sunday at noon it is filled with believers who recite the Angelus or the Regina Coeli together with the Pope who appears at the second last window of the top floor of the building on the right; they listen to his words and receive his blessing. On Wednesdays, multitudes of pilgrims of every nationality, age and walk of life cross the square to reach the "Paul VI Audience Hall" where the Pope receives them at the General Audience. On special occasions it is moving to be able to take part in this same square in solemn Eucharistic celebrations or ecumenical prayer meetings together with the Supreme Pontiff, cardinals and bishops, the pastors of other Churches and the

The granite obelisk in the center of the square

people of God, an immense multitude of every nation, race, people and tongue (cf. Rv 7:9). It can certainly be said that in St. Peter's Square the Church's nature is particularly evident: a people of God who recognize him in the truth and serve him with a life of holiness.

In the 18th and 19th centuries, an attempt was made to integrate St. Peter's Square within a broader urbanization context, but the final decision which led to its present situation was taken by Pius XI (1922-1939) alone. It was he who approved the plan to pull down the old buildings between Borgo Vecchio and Borgo Nuovo. The demolition began in 1937 and ended in time for the Holy Year in 1950, when the Via della Conciliazione was inaugurated.

The obelisk and fountains in St. Peter's Square

A large pink granite *obelisk* can be admired in the center of the square. It was hewn from a single block and stands 25.31 m. high on a base 8.25 m. wide. This obelisk which comes from Helio-

View of the basilica's dome

polis, Egypt, where it was built by the Pharaoh Mencares in 1835 BC in honor of the sun, was brought to Rome in 37 BC by the Emperor Caligula (37-41) and erected in the circus he built. Here it was the silent witness of the martyrdom of St. Peter and of many other Christians. In 1586 Sixtus V had it moved to the center of St. Peter's Square. This operation, which required hundreds of workmen, was directed by Domenico Fontana with the help of his brother, Giovanni, and took four months. It was erected on September 10, 1586 by 900 men using 140 horses and 44 winches. A pagan monument erected in the greatest Christian square, the obelisk is a symbol of humanity reaching to Christ. Two sides of the obelisk were originally inscribed with dedications to the "divine Augustus" and to the "divine Tiberius". Sixtus V dedicated it to the Holy Cross,

and had engraved on it the inscription: "Christus vincit, Christus regnat, Christus imperat". The obelisk stands between *two monumental fountains,* 14 m. high, symbols of Christ, the source of living water for eternal life. The fountain on the right is the work of Carlo Maderno (1613). Bernini, who designed the square, had it erected where it now stands, and for purposes of symmetry built the fountain on the left (1675).

Between the obelisk and the fountains are two porphyry discs set into the pavement which mark the two centers of the ellipse. Additional discs of white marble are arranged along the meridian line, linked with the circle surrounding the obelisk and set between the wedge-shaped cobblestones known as "sampietrini" which pave the whole square. In this circle are indicated the cardinal points of the compass and the figures of the Zodiac.

Statue of St. Paul wielding the sword; he is also holding a parchment scroll

PIVS · IX · P · M ·

The dome (exterior)

From the square, we can admire the grandiose *dome of St. Peter's*. It was planned and designed by Michelangelo who directed work on it to the level of the drum. Giacomo Della Porta completed the task. He increased its span by 7 m. in comparison to the original plans thereby giving it a greater impetus. The dome, almost 137 m. high, can be seen from every part of Rome and has become the city's symbol.

On the outside of the basilica and dome, Michelangelo designed a continuous, level wall which surrounds the whole building. This gigantic wall in a single order punctuated by windows and niches, is surmounted by an attic with windows. Above this structure is the drum and the final arch of the dome.

Statues of Christ the Redeemer, St. John the Baptist and one of the Apostles which crown the basilica's façade

The façade

A flight of 39 steps divided by three platforms leads to the parvis. At the foot of the steps are *two statues:* on the left, *St. Peter,* and on the right, *St. Paul,* sculpted by G. Fabris and A. Todolini in 1840 and erected there in 1847 by Pius IX, replacing two smaller statues.

The noble and dignified *façade,* as we have mentioned, is the work of Carlo Maderno. He wanted it rather low (45.50 m.) in comparison to its breadth (117.70 m.) in order not to obscure the view of the vast dome. The travertine marble façade is divided by eight gigantic columns, 27 m. high with a diameter of almost 3 m., and four pilaster strips in Corinthian style, which support the entablature. Above it is the attic,

The left-hand clock with the bell blessed by Pius VI in 1786

with rectangular windows, surmounted by a balustrade, on which stand *13 statues,* 5.70 m. tall, portraying *Christ the Redeemer,* eternally alive in his Church, *St. John the Baptist,* precursor of Jesus, and 11 Apostles (the statues of St. Peter and St. Paul are at the foot of the steps).

The façade is flanked by *two 18th century clocks,* built by Giuseppe Valadier. The one on the left shows the exact time in Rome, and the one on the

The "Mater Ecclesiae" mosaic, commissioned by Pope John Paul II, commemorating the attempt to assassinate him

right, which has a single hand, European mean time. They recall that the Church lives on in time and that Christ will be with her until the end of time.

Beneath the clock on the left is the *campanone* (great bell) of St. Peter's, which has a diameter of 2.50 m., a height of 2.60 m. and weighs 440.92 lbs. It was cast by Luigi Valadier and blessed by Pius VI in 1786. It is rung at Christmas, at Easter, on the Solemnity of Sts. Peter and Paul, and every time the Pope imparts the "Urbi et Orbi" blessing (to the city and to the world).

On the entablature is a Latin inscription in enormous letters: "In honorem Principis Apostoli Paolus V Burghesius Romanus Pont. Max. anno MDCXII - Pont. VII" (in honor of the Prince of the Apostles Paul V Borghese, Supreme Roman Pontiff, in the year 1612, the 7th year of his pontificate).

There are nine loggias between the columns and the pilasters of the façade. In the center the Loggia of the Blessings stands out. It is from here that the election of the new Pope is announced with the famous words: "Nuntio vobis gaudium magnum. Habemus Papam!"; and from here the new Pope imparts his first "Urbi et Orbi" blessing which he renews on the solemnities of Easter and Christmas. Above the central loggia is a tympanum in the classical style; beneath it is the famous high relief portraying the consignment of the keys, by Ambrogio Bonvicino (1552-1622). It shows Jesus who is saying to Peter: "I will entrust to you the keys of the kingdom of heaven. Whatever you declare bound on earth shall be bound in heaven; whatever you declare loosed on earth shall be loosed in heaven" (Mt 16:19).

Interior of the portico

Equestrian statue of Charlemagne, at the left end of the portico

Equestrian statue of Constantine, at the right end of the portico

The portico

The *portico* [1] is reached from the parvis through five entrances. Above the central door is the coat of arms of Paul V Borghese, above the two middle doorways that of Urban VIII Barberini, and above the two outer doors on the far sides, is that of Paul VI Braschi.

Stone tablets on the walls which support the central entrance and the two middle doorways recall the proclamation of the dogma of the Assumption of Mary into Heaven, defined by Pius XII on 1 November 1950.

The portico, large, solemn and bright, is the masterpiece of Carlo Maderno (1556-1629). It is 71 m. long, 13.50 m. wide and 20 m. high.

The wall of the basilica is divided by six pilasters and Ionic columns. The pavement of precious marbles, initially designed by Bernini, was restored under Leo XIII in 1880. In the central section, Pope John XXIII's coat of arms commemorates the inauguration of the Second Vatican Council on October 11, 1962.

The vault of the portico is decorated in stucco reliefs by Martino Ferrabosco. It shows Paul V's coat of arms and episodes from the Acts of the Apostles. The stucco statues next to it in the lunettes of the vault, show the first 32 martyred popes.

At the left end of the portico is the *equestrian statue of Charlemagne*, the first emperor to be crowned in St. Peter's (on Christmas Eve, in the year 800), made in 1725 by Agostino Cornacchini (1685-1740); at the other end on the right, is *the equestrian statue of Constantine*, made by Bernini (1598-1680) in 1670, and considered one of his masterpieces. The two straight wings, as we have said, are named after these two statues which are 139 m. apart.

Opposite the central entrance as one turns to look toward the square, high up in the lunette is the *"Navicella Mosaic"*, attributed to Giotto (1266-1337). Only fragments remain of the original hung here in 1675, when a copy of the artist's work was made. The mosaic shows Jesus who is walking on the waters of the Sea of Tiberias and inviting Peter to come to him. But Peter, letting himself be overcome by fear is beginning to sink. Jesus saves him and says "How little faith you have!... Why did you falter?" (Mt 14:24-31).

Mosaic of the "Navicella", attributed to Giotto

The doors

Five doors, corresponding to the five naves of the ancient and new buildings, give access to the basilica. Four of them are the work of contemporary artists, as a witness of the perennial vitality of the Church and her capacity to awaken artistic inspiration in all ages. The scenes portrayed on the doors invite the visitor to reflect on the significance of the building he is about to enter, and on the meaning of his visit to the basilica.

The *first door on the left* is called the *Door of Death* [2] because at one time it was the exit for funeral processions. The scenes sculpted between 1961 and 1964 by Giacomo Manzù (1908-1991) in accordance with the wishes of John XXIII (1958-1963), express the Christian meaning of death in ten episodes. Above right: the *Death of Jesus;* the death of the Just who redeems and saves us; above left: the *Death of Mary* who is immediately borne to heaven, a sign of the sure hope of resurrection for all humankind. In the center, a vine branch (left) and some ears of wheat (right). From the ground grains of wheat and the pressed grapes are made the bread and wine which in the Eucharist become the

Door of Death,
by Giacomo Manzù

Door of Good and Evil, by Luciano Minguzzi

bread of life and the drink of salvation. Below left: the *Violent death of the innocent Abel*, for whom God asks his brother Cain to account, and the *Serene death of St. Joseph*, patron of all who desire a holy death, the *Death of the first Pope, St. Peter*, hanging on the cross, but upside down, since he felt unworthy to die like his Lord, and the *Death of Pope John XXIII*, the good parish priest of the world whose death deeply affected people of all religions and nationalities; below right: the *Death of the Proto-martyr, St. Stephen*, killed by those who had killed Jesus and, who like Jesus, prayed for and forgave his executioners;

and the *Death of Pope Gregory VII*, who died in exile because he "loved justice and hated irreverence", defending the Church against the emperor's claims. Finally, *Death improvised in space* and the *Death of the mother at home* in front of the child she abandons. Under the panels are six creatures: a blackbird, a dormouse, a hedgehog, an owl, a tortoise and a raven. On the inside of the door can be seen the impression of Manzù's hand and a portrayal of John XXIII receiving the bishops on the first day of the Second Vatican Council, October 11, 1962.

The *second door*, the work of Luciano

Central Door,
by Antonio Averulino,
known as Filarete

Minguzzi, who worked on it from 1970 to 1977, is the *Door of Good and Evil* [**3**]. The artist donated it to Pope Paul VI (1963-1978) on his 80th birthday. On the right panel: *Goodness* is shown. *St. Augustine* silences a Manichaean heretic, because the truth must triumph over error; *a pair of doves* nesting are a reminder that love generates peace; *Baptism* which was grafted in Jesus enables us to do good: *the un-armed soldier who is receiving communion from a black cardinal* recalls what the true weapons of good are. *John XXIII and Paul VI together with the three cardinal moderators* represent the Church meet-ing in Council to seek the best ways to help man achieve his own good; *Lazarus rising from his tomb* shows what man's final good is, while *the young Tobias accompanied by the Angel Raphael* assures us that God leads us on the way of goodness.

On the left panel, *Evil* is depicted: hatred of the faith leads to the *martyrdom of Sts. Vitalis and Agricola,* the slave and the master; *a falcon kills a dove; the crucifixion of St. Andrew and the maltreatment of the slaves; torture and killing for religious or political reasons* are inspired by the devil; *Cain killing Abel and the unrepentant thief* who *insulted Jesus and was crucified with him,* are slaves of evil.

The *central door* [4] is the oldest. Pope Eugene IV commissioned the Florentine, Antonio Averulino, known as Filarete (1400-1469) to make the two bronze imposts which he completed in 1445. The six panels show: *Jesus the Savior* and *Mary* enthroned, the two centers of Christian piety, then as now; *St. Paul* with the sword, the weapon with which he was beheaded and whose blade is double-edged like God's words, and *St. Peter,* who is giving the keys to the kneeling Pope Eugene IV, are the two pillars of the Church of Rome. The two

lowest panels show St. Paul sentenced by Nero and the *martyrdom of St. Paul,* who kneels as, blindfold, he awaits the stroke of the sword that will take his life, and *the martyrdom of St. Peter,* dragged to the Vatican Hill where he is crucified. St. Paul then appears to Plautilla, to give her back the veil she had lent him to blindfold his eyes. The bas-reliefs between the framed panels show scenes from the pontificate of Eugene IV, and representatives at the Council of Ferrara-Florence, summoned in 1438 to reunite the Churches of the East and of the West.

On the right of the main entrance is

Door of the Sacraments, by Venanzio Crocetti

The Holy Door,
by Vico Consorti

the *fourth door,* made by Venanzio Crocetti (1965), called the "Door of the Sacraments" [5]. It is 7.43 meters high and 3.80 m. wide, and consists of two leaves of four panels each. These show the seven sacraments, signs of the faith and sources of grace, actions with which Jesus saves us. In the panels on the left: the angel announces the grace of the sacraments: Baptism, Confirmation and Penance; in the panels on the right: the Eucharist, Marriage, Holy Orders, and the Anointing of the Sick.

The last door on the right is the "Holy Door" [6]. This door is bricked up on the inside. On first day of the Holy Year the Pope strikes the brick wall with a hammer, and so opens the door to let in the pilgrims who come to make the most of the indulgence. It will be closed by the Pope himself at the end of the Holy Year. The Holy Door represents Jesus, the Good Shepherd and the gate of the sheep pen: "I am the gate. Whoever enters through me, will be safe. He will go in and out, and find pasture" (Jn 10:9). The Holy Year is celebrated every 25 years. In this century two extraordinary Holy Years of Redemption have also been celebrated on the anniversary of Jesus' death on the Cross: 1933 and 1983. When the wall is knocked down, the bronze panels of the door made by Vico Consorti appear. Since 24 December 1949 they have replaced the former wooden panels made in 1749. This door is also called the "Door of the Great Pardon". Its panels portray scenes of man's sin and his redemption through God's mercy: 1. Through disobedience Adam and Eve turned away from God and happiness and were chased from the garden; Mary receives the announcement of salvation from the angel and directs humanity back to God. 2. Through Baptism, Jesus permits us to join his People; he comes to seek us when we stray from him, as the shepherd goes in search of his lost sheep; he awaits our return and welcomes us at the door, as the father welcomes the prodigal son; he cures those who are paralyzed by sin. 3. Jesus opens the door of new life to the woman who is sinful but can love; Jesus tells Peter says that one must forgive seventy times seven times. Jesus trusts anew in the man who promises fidelity and then denies him, Jesus opens the door of heaven to the thief who calls on him. 4. Jesus unlocks the heart of doubting Thomas to the faith; he gives his Spirit to the Apostles to enable them to forgive sins; he tumbles Paul from his horse and suddenly opens up a whole new world to him; he knocks at everyone's door and waits for us to open it.

St. Peter's Basilica, the Pope's cathedral

On entering the central nave [7], we might well wonder what a church is. It is well known that the first Christians met in one another's homes to pray. Only in the fourth century did they start to make permanently available for worship cer-

tain buildings that were called churches, that is, places destined to receive the "Ecclesia", a word which means "a summoned gathering". Various kinds of churches have different names: basilica, cathedral, parish church, temple, shrine.

The name "basilica" is the architectural term for the rectangular building used by the ancient Romans for their legal proceedings. The Christians of Rome held their gatherings in this type of building which is why Rome's most important churches are called basilicas.

The church which is the bishop's seat, where he gathers his flock, is called a cathedral. (A parish church is one where the parish priest, appointed by the bishop, gathers the faithful who live in that specific parish). The Bishop of Rome's cathedral is the Basilica of St. John Lateran.

Here, as Bishop of Rome, the Pope gathers Rome's Christians. However, as Successor of Peter, he also exercises spiritual sovereignty over all the Church and in his capacity as Head of the whole Church, he has chosen to carry out his ministry in the Vatican palaces and to gather the faithful of the whole world in St. Peter's Basilica.

For several centuries the popes alternated between the two basilicas, but with Nicholas V (1447-1455), the Vatican definitively became the Pope's residence. This is why St. Peter's Basilica is considered the Pope's church and therefore somehow everyone's church, the cathedral of the world, the place which symbolically unites all Christians.

In St. Peter's Basilica the Pope exercises the functions which Jesus bequeathed to his Apostles: the roles of teaching, sanctifying and governing.

The Pope teaches frequently in this basilica, and in some cases exceptionally, for example when "as supreme

An assembly of Bishops meeting for the Council in St Peter's, in the Holy Father's presence

pastor and teacher of all the faithful ... he proclaims in an absolute decision a doctrine pertaining to faith or morals" (*Lumen gentium,* n. 25). In these cases he enjoys the prerogative of infallibility, which "is also present in the body of bishops when, with Peter's successor, they exercise the supreme teaching office" (ibid.), that is, when they meet in council. The two last ecumenical councils, (the First and Second Vatican Councils) were celebrated precisely in St. Peter's Basilica. In addition, the Pope "canonizes" saints in St. Peter's, that is he decrees that a "Servant of God" who has already been beatified (proclaimed blessed), should be added to the list of saints and venerated in the universal Church.

By this act the Pope declares in an infallible way that a person enjoys heavenly glory, and above all, shows that sainthood is an essential element in the life of the Church and that in every age there are members of the People of God in whom heroic holiness can be tangibly observed. The first "canonization" recorded as having taken place in St. Peter's Basilica was St. Bridget's, celebrated on October 7, 1391.

In St. Peter's Basilica the Church exercises her *sanctifying role.* Here all the sacraments are celebrated, and it is often the Pope who presides. The *Eucharist* is solemnly celebrated at the Altars of the Chair and of the Confessio, occasionally also at the basilica's numerous other altars, and at fixed times in two chapels where the Blessed Sacrament is preserved for adoration. The faithful who enter the church never fail to spend a few minutes praying before the tabernacle.

Many Christians have been *baptized* in this basilica. Many have also received *confirmation* here. On some occasions the Pope himself has blessed the *marriage* of Christian couples. Many bishops have been able to receive their *episcopal consecration* here from the Supreme Pontiff's hands, a most obvious expression of their link with the Bishop of Rome. Here too, numerous priests have been able to receive their *priestly ordination* from the Pope himself. Lastly, the sacrament of *reconciliation* is also celebrated in this basilica. The faithful may have recourse to it at all hours and find a priest who speaks their language here at all times. On Good Friday, the Pope himself enters a confessional and exercises this ministry for several hours. In St. Peter's Basilica several *important acts of government* also take place.

It is here that the Pope usually announces important events. Here the Pope confers the insignia of their rank to the cardinals he has chosen as his co-workers in the governance of the Church. Here the new Pope, elected by the cardinals a few days earlier in the Sistine Chapel, begins his ministry as Supreme Pastor of the Church.

Those who enter St. Peter's Basilica come here first and foremost to pray, to strengthen their will to follow the teaching of the Apostles and to pay the homage of obedience to the Successor of Peter whose duty it is to maintain the bond of unity, charity and peace within the Church.

Visitors can also admire the basilica's magnificent artistic masterpieces that have inspired artists of all ages and all places, and contemplate the various historical memorials. However, their conduct must always be properly respectful for a sacred place and they cannot visit the basilica as tourists during important celebrations. This guide, in which we now briefly present the major artistic monuments should be understood in this light.

The opening ceremony of the Second Vatican Council

GROUND PLAN
OF ST. PETER'S
BASILICA

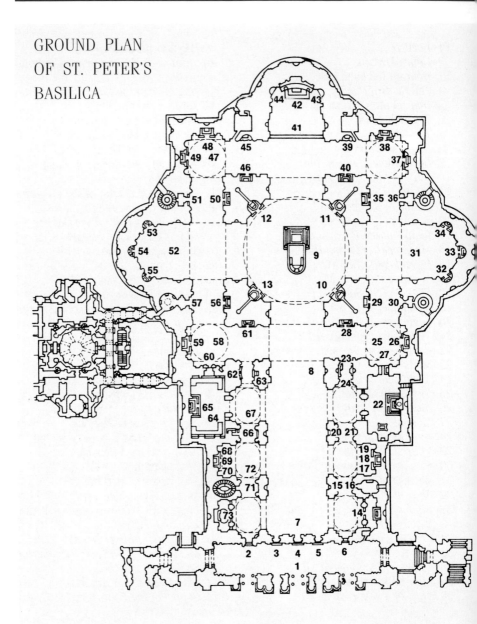

The interior
of St. Peter's Basilica

The *plan* of the basilica *is in the form of a Latin cross*. That is, the vertical or upright bar, constituted by the central nave and two lateral naves, is longer than the horizontal one formed by the transept. Marking the point of their intersection are the four massive piers which support the dome and in the center is the papal altar.

When they enter the basilica, visitors immediately pause for an instant at the beginning of the central nave to enjoy the ecstatic view of grandeur and the solemnity and peace which the basilica inspires. Despite the vast size of the structures and the splendor of the decorations, one has the impression of entering a place of prayer and recollection. One cannot but feel admiration for the "magnanimity" of those who conceived, commissioned, planned and built a church on such a grand scale, perhaps out of proportion for their time, but worthy of the immense crowds which have filled and fill it so frequently and which they prophetically foresaw.

Here, at the beginning of the central nave, one immediately realizes that the immense basilica was built to safeguard two precious heirlooms: the tomb of St. Peter and his Chair. The famous "baldacchino" (canopy) over the Altar of the Confessio and the sumptuous Altar of the Chair direct the pilgrim's gaze to these two treasures.

The central nave

In this nave [7] seats were installed for the Council Fathers who celebrated the Second Vatican Ecumenical Council here from 1962 to 1965. As far as the third pilaster it was built by Carlo Maderno. It is 45 m. high (137 beneath the dome) 27 m. wide (140 m. in the transept) and 187 m. long. It is bordered by three couples of massive pilasters, with Corinthian pilaster strips. Above the pilasters are six arches (three on each side) which support the long trabeation under the barrel vault enhanced with late 18th-century coffers during the pontificate of Pope Pius VI.

On the trabeation which extends the whole length of the basilica is a *Latin text* in large black letters on a gold-background. On the left, starting from the back it reads: "Ego rogavi pro te, o Petre, ut non deficiat fides tua: et tu aliquando conversus confirma fratres tuos" ("I have prayed for you, Peter, that your faith may never fail; and you in turn must strengthen your brothers" (Lk 22:32). On the right, starting above the statue of St. Peter and extending to the back wall, are the words: "Quodcumque ligaveris super terram, erit ligatum et in coelis: et quodcumque solveris super terram, erit solutum et in coelis" (I will entrust to you the keys of the kingdom of heaven. Whatever you declare bound on earth shall be bound in heaven; and whatever you declare loosed on earth shall be loosed in heaven) (Mt 16:19).

At the beginning of the central nave the visitors' gaze is attracted *to two holy water stoups* that provide a clue to the basilica's real size: the cupids which seem small are in fact 2 m. tall. The basins containing the holy water are the work of Francesco Moderati (1680-1721) and A. Cornacchini (1685-1740) (on the left); and by Giuseppe Lironi (1668-1749) and G.B. De Rossi (on the right). They offer the holy water so that those who enter may make the sign of the cross, in memory of their own baptism.

Close to the entrance to this nave a great *disc of red porphyry* stands out against the marble paving. It comes from the old basilica, where it was located near the main altar. Kneeling on it, the Emperor Charlemagne was crowned Emperor by Pope Leo III, at Christmas in the year 800. Another 21 emperors subsequently knelt on this same disc to receive the crown of the Holy Roman Empire from the Pope's hands.

As they proceed, visitors are curious to observe the measurements of the 15 largest churches in the world recorded in brass letters on the pavement. Toward the center of the nave, the Holy Year of the Redemption proclaimed by Pius XI in

1933 is also recalled by an inscription on the floor.

The nave was decorated by Gian Lorenzo Bernini, who was commissioned by Innocent X in 1645 to complete the decoration of the pilasters and chapels. He and his assistants are therefore responsible for the various *decorations:* the cherubs, the doves and the symbols of the papacy such as the tiara and the keys.

On the inner sides of the colossal pilasters, between the pilaster strips are two sequences of *niches* which contain 39 statues of the founders of religious orders and congregations, placed here as from the beginning of the 18th cen-

Statue of a holy founder, St. Peter of Alcantara

tury. Many of their faces are familiar to us. They all remind us to live the Gospel and to follow Jesus. On the right, starting at the entrance are: St. Theresa of Jesus (below) and St. Sofia Maddalena Barat (above), St. Vincent de Paul and St. John Eudes, St. Philip Neri and St. John Baptist de la Salle, St. John Bosco (above the statue of St. Peter). On the left are: St. Peter of Alcantara and St. Lucia Filippini, St. Camillo de Lellis, St. Louis Grignion de Montfort, St. Ignatius of Loyola, St. Antony Mary Zaccaria, St. Francis de Paola, St. Peter Fourier. As we shall see later, the statues of saints continue in the transept.

Decorations on a chapel pilaster

Bronze statue of St. Peter, dressed in solemn robes

The *bronze statue of St. Peter* [8] stands out among the ornamentations of the central nave. Close to the first pier on the right supporting the dome, it shows us St. Peter seated on a marble throne in the act of blessing the faithful with his right hand, while in his left he holds the keys of the kingdom. On 29 June, the Feast of St. Peter, the statue is dressed in solemn vestments. It has been attributed to Arnolfo di Cambio (1245-1302) but, it seems, erroneously. In fact a seal dated 1283 was found which shows this statue, and the epigraph beneath it describes it as "ancient". It is probable that it is an early sixth-century work which ended up in the basilica in 1300. St. Peter's throne was made in 1800, and stands on a Sicilian jasper pedestal made in the mid-18th century. The two candelabra were placed in front of the statue in 1971.

Above the canopy made in 1871, a circular mosaic portrays Pius IX (1847-1878) who granted an indulgence to those who kissed the foot of the statue. In fact, it is still the tradition for pilgrims to kiss St. Peter's now worn right foot, after praying in front of the statue.

The Confessio and the papal altar

We have now reached the intersection of the transept and the central nave [9], the place known as the *Confessio*, that is, where St. Peter witnessed to his faith with his martyrdom. It already existed in the ancient basilica but was enlarged

and embellished with marble by Maderno (1556-1629). It is horseshoe-shaped like an exedra and bordered by a balustrade before which the faithful kneel to confess their faith, reciting the *Creed* or *Apostolic Symbol*, that is, the 12 articles of faith which date back to the Apostles. All along the balustrade are 93 perpetually burning oil lamps arranged on artistic cornucopia, symbols of the faith and love of the Christian people.

Two broad stairways in Greek marble, at the end of which are two small statues of St. Peter and St. Paul, give access to a lower area, on the level of the Constantinian basilica. In the center of a sumptuous wall divided by a richly gilded gate is a *sacellum*, beneath which is St. Peter's tomb. Here the memory of Peter has always been venerated, and it is here that a graffitto in Greek was found which says, "Peter is here". Pilgrims come here from all over the world to "see Peter", and to pray by his tomb.

Next to it, in boxes protected by a sheet of glass, are the bones found in recent excavations at the foot of "wall G". On June 26, 1968, Paul VI was able to say: "new extremely patient and accurate investigations have been made, so that reassured by the opinion of the competent persons who are skilled and careful, we believe the result to be positive: the relics of St. Peter have been identified in a way we can accept as convincing".

At the center of the *sacellum* the "niche of the palliums" is visible. In it is kept the bronze coffer that contains the palliums, that is, narrow white stoles woven from the wool of the lambs blessed on the feast of St. Agnes (January 21) and embroidered with black crosses, which the Pope bestows upon patriarchs and metropolitans as a permanent reminder of the Church's unity.

The Confessio and the Papal Altar

The back wall of the *sacellum* is decorated with an 11th-century mosaic depicting Christ the Savior.

Next to the Confessio in the center of the basilica stands the high or papal altar, commonly known as the *Altar of the Confessio*. It was carved from a gigantic block of Greek marble which lay in Nerva's Forum, and consecrated by Clement VIII on June 26, 1594. It is set on an older altar erected by Callistus II in 1123, which in turn contains another even older one.

The altar is surmounted by the splendid, majestic bronze "baldacchino", Bernini's first work in the basilica. He took nine years to make it, from 1624 to 1633, and used 6,200 k. of metal. The monument is typical of the 17th-century style: it stands on four pedestals of marble on which in the papal escutcheons a wonderful sequence showing "motherhood" is carved, liberally scattered with the heraldic bees of the Barberini to whose family Pope Urban VIII belonged. It was he who had commissioned Bernini to make this canopy in 1624. It rests upon *four gigantic twisted columns*, 20 m. high, adorned with sprigs of olive and bay, among which the graceful figures of cherubs appear. Acanthus leaves en-

Niche of the Palliums beneath the papal altar

Two twisted columns adorned with olive branches and bay leaves

Capitals and crosses, decorating the "Baldacchino"

twine the base and the capitals. The spiral fluting of the columns suggests upward movement. Like the portable canopies used in processions to cover the Eucharist, fringes and tassels dangle from the top of the covering. Inside the "ciborium" is a dove, the symbol of the Holy Spirit, in a burst of golden rays. Above the frieze on each capital, four angels, the work of François du Duquesnoy, offer garlands, while between them couples of smaller angels support the Pope's emblems: the keys, the tiara, the book and the sword. The vertex, where four vast ribs and palm branches converge from the four corners, is crowned by the cross, set on a golden globe.

The dome (interior)

The great dome soars above the altar and the baldacchino, sumptuously embellished with mosaic and stucco ornaments. It is supported by four structural piers with a perimeter of 71 m. and a height of 120 m. from the ground to the roof of the lantern.

The giant letters on a gold background, from St. Veronica to St. Helen, say "Hinc una fides mundo refulget" (From here a single faith shines throughout the world); and from St. Longinus to St. Andrew: "Hinc sacerdotii unitas exoritur" (From here is born the unity of the priesthood).

In the *four spandrels* which link the square piers and the circular drum, the four Evangelists are portrayed in medallions with a diameter of 8.5 m.: Matthew with the ox, Mark with the lion, Luke with the angel and John with the eagle.

Around the base of the drum we can read the solemn words from Matthew's Gospel with which Jesus invests Peter with supreme authority. The text reads: "Tu es Petrus et super hanc petram aedificabo ecclesiam meam et tibi dabo claves regni caelorum" (You are 'Rock' and on this rock I will build my Church, to you I will give the keys of the kingdom of heaven") (Mt 16:18).

1. busts of the 16 popes buried in the basilica;

2. majestic figures of Christ, the Virgin Mary, St. Joseph, St. John the Baptist and various Apostles;

3. in the rectangular frames, angels bearing the instruments of Jesus' Passion;

4. the faces of cherubim and seraphim in circular medallions;

5. angels, the custodians of St. Peter's tomb;

6. additional faces of winged angels. Above the 96 figures is a blue sky spangled with stars, and above it the lantern at whose base is a Latin inscription: "To the glory of St. Peter, Pope Sixtus V in the year 1590, the fifth of his pontificate".

The eye then penetrates the lantern which is 18 m. long, and as in a vision comes to rest on the glorious figure of God the Father.

Many artists worked on these decorations. Clement VIII commissioned Giuseppe Cesari, known as Cavalier d'Arpino (1568-1640) to carry out the upper part of the decoration. He prepared the cartoons from 1603 to 1612. His drawings were simultaneously transposed into mosaic by the best mosaic artists of the period

The gigantic black letters (2 m. high) of this text on a gold background are lit by the light from 16 large windows, typical of Michelangelo's style, which punctuate the drum.

Above the windows, the dome is divided into sixteen ribs and as many segments, decorated by majestic figures on six ascending concentric levels.

Starting at the bottom the figures portray:

The octagon with the piers and the Loggias of the Relics

The dome above the papal altar is supported by four gigantic *piers*, 45 m. high with a perimeter of 71 m., started by Bramante and completed by Michelangelo. In 1624 Urban VIII

St. Longinus

commissioned Bernini to create four loggias in these piers. They are called the "Loggias of the Relics". Each is protected by a balustrade and adorned with two columns decorated with vine leaves and splendid bas-reliefs referring to the four "major relics". In fact, Urban VIII wanted him to carve out four niches in these loggias, where he then had placed the precious relics, formerly kept but not properly preserved in the basilica.

The *relics* were: several fragments of the Cross of Jesus, which were found in the Roman churches of Santa Croce in Gerusalemme and Santa Anastasia, which in 1629 Urban VIII wished to be given to St. Peter's Basilica and placed in the pier of St. Helen; a scrap of material, showing the imprint of the face of a bearded man which had been brought by the crusades from Jerusalem to Rome and was already venerated

Loggia of the Relics

St. Helen

St. Veronica

before the 12th century; a fragment of the lance which was said to have belonged to St. Longinus and which Sultan Bajazet, the son of Mahomet II, had presented to Pope Innocent VIII (1492); St. Andrew's head, brought to Venice by Thomas Palaiologos and donated to Pius II (1460).

The relics are now no longer in their original site, but the three relics of Our Lord's Passion are kept in the chapel above the statue of St. Veronica, and displayed to the people on the fifth Sunday in Lent. The relic of St. Andrew's head however, was sent by Paul VI as a gift to the Church of St. Andrew in Patras and a sign of friendship with the Greek Orthodox Church.

Beneath the loggias of the relics Bernini created huge niches which hold four colossal statues, almost 10 m. high, which are associated with the relics. In the first pier on the right is the statue of

St. Andrew

St. Longinus [10], the soldier who pierced the side of Jesus, from which "blood and water" flowed. It was carved by Bernini in 1643 from four blocks of marble. The second pier contains the statue of St. Helen [11], mother of the Emperor Constantine, to whose devotion we owe the discovery of fragments of Jesus' holy cross. The statue was made in 1646 by Andrea Bolgi from several blocks of marble. The third pier contains the statue of St. Veronica [12], the woman who according to tradition wiped Jesus' face with a linen cloth as he heaved the cross toward Calvary. It was made by Francesco Mocchi (1580-1654) from three blocks of marble, before 1632. The fourth pier contains the statue of St. Andrew [13], St. Peter's brother, who evangelized Greece. The statue is the work of François Duquesnoy (1594-1643). It was made from a single block of marble and erected in 1639.

Beneath the piers is the entrance which leads down a flight of steps to the Vatican Grottos which pilgrims visit once they have completed their tour of the basilica.

The entrance under the statue of St. Longinus is usually open.

The side aisles

We can now return to the basilica's entrance and walk down the side aisles. Like the central nave they are the work (as far as the central pilasters) of Carlo Maderno, who made them in accordance with the architectural and liturgical norms of the day: a series of communicating chapels embellished with precious works of art. On the inside of the six arches, are portraits of the first 56 canonized popes in marble medal-

Beginning of the right-hand nave, with the Holy Door seen from the inside

lions, supported by cherubs. They alternate with the coats of arms of Innocent X whose emblem was the dove. The architectural structures of the aisles are decorated with 44 Cottanello marble columns with architraves, tympanums, and statuary groups.

Walking down the aisles, visitors should not forget to take a look at the ten minor cupolas: six elliptical, above the lateral aisles, and four circular, above the four corner chapels.

The right aisle

In the right aisle, after the Holy Door and seen from the interior, the first chapel we reach is the *Chapel of the Pietà* [14] which was initially called the Chapel of the Crucifix. In fact, in this chapel Giovanni Lanfranco (1582-1647), using the fresco technique, decorated the walls with eight *episodes of Christ's Passion,* and on the central vault above the altar he painted the *Exaltation of the Cross.* Other mosaics also decorate the vault, spandrels and lunettes.

But the most famous monument in the chapel is the marble group of the *Pietà* by Michelangelo (1475-1564). He sculpted it from a single block of white Carrara marble in 1498-1499, when he was not yet 25 years old. Originally destined for the Chapel of St. Petronilla, for the tomb of Cardinal Jean de Bilhères who commissioned it, it was moved to St. Peter's Basilica and only in 1736 placed in this chapel on the base made by Francesco Borromini in 1626.

Monument to Queen
Christina of Sweden

It portrays the devout gesture of Mary who bears the lifeless body of her Son in her lap. There are no realistic wounds, no hopeless grief is shown, but a composed, serene and heavenly sorrow. The still youthful face of Mary, gently inclined over the body of her dead Son reminded the artist of the face of his mother who died when he was five years old. It reminds Christians that the face of the Virgin Mary was never spoilt by any wrinkle of age or stain of sin, nor even by death. It also represents the ever youthful, unmarked face of the Church, bride and mother, and prefigures the face of the children of the resurrection who have reached the heavenly fatherland. Christians who contemplate Michelangelo's masterpiece think of the mystery of Christ's death and resurrection and invoke the Blessed Virgin Mary.

The Pietà

On the band crossing Mary's breast is Michelangelo's signature: "Michangelo Bonarotus Floren. faciebat". In 1972, after a lunatic disfigured Mary's face on the morning of May 20, 1971, the monument was restored and is now protected by a special glass screen.

Returning to the nave, we come across two funeral monuments. On the left against the pilaster facing the central nave is the *Monument to Christina of Sweden* [**15**] by Carlo Fontana (1634-1714). The Queen is shown in a gilt and bronze medallion, supported by a crowned skull. There are three reliefs on the urn: Christina relinquishes the throne of Sweden to embrace Catholicism (center), the scorn of the nobility

(on the right), faith which triumphs over heresy (on the left).

Opposite is the *Monument to Leo XII* [**16**] (1823-1829), who is shown in the act of giving his blessing for the Jubilee of 1825. It was executed by G. de Fabris (1790-1860). Above the statue, two reclining figures (*Religion* and *Justice*) support the coat of arms. It should be noted that this is not a real funeral monument because the Pontiff's body is buried in front of the altar of St. Leo the Great. Beneath this monument is a door, usually closed, which leads into a small elliptical chapel. This was at first called the *Chapel of the Relics* or *of the Crucifix*, because it contains a wooden crucifix, attributed to Pietro Cavallini, a

Chapel of St. Sebastian

13th-century Roman artist. It then became known as St. Nicholas' Chapel because although one of its two altars is dedicated to St. Joseph, the other, with a mosaic of the saint made in 1711, is dedicated to St. Nicholas of Bari.

The *Chapel of St. Sebastian*, [**18**] named after the subject of the mosaic above the altar, immediately follows. It was completed by Pier Paolo Cristofari after a drawing by Domenico Zampieri, better known as Domenichino (1581-

1641). Below the altar the body of Bl. Innocent XI (1676-1689) is preserved in a crystal casket.

In this chapel we also find two modern works. On the right is the *statue of Pius XI* [**17**] (1922-1939), the first sovereign of Vatican City State which was created in 1929 as a result of the Lateran Pact. The statue was made by Francesco Nagni (1897-1977) in 1949.

On the left is the *statue of Pius XII* (1939-1958) [**19**], commissioned by the

Cardinals he had created, and made by Francesco Messina in 1964. The Pope is shown blessing the faithful, clad in papal robes. His gesture also seems to express his desire to put an end to the scourge of the Second World War, while his expression seems to reiterate his famous sentence: "Nothing is lost with peace, all can be lost with war".

In the aisle, in the archway between the second and third chapels, we find another two monuments. On the left, the *funeral monument of Countess Matilda di Canossa*, [20] Pope Gregory VII's great champion against the Emperor Henry IV. The monument was conceived by Bernini who began it in 1633. The statue of Matilda is by Andrea Bolgi (1605-1656). The central bas-relief which shows Henry IV kneeling before Gregory VII on 28 January 1077 after waiting for three days and three nights to be received, is the work of Stefano Speranza. The two cherubs supporting

Also on the right is the vast *Chapel of the Blessed Sacrament* [**22**], behind a Baroque wrought-iron grill designed by Francesco Borromini (1599-1667). The Blessed Sacrament is exposed here for the continuous adoration of the faithful. A notice reads: "Only those who wish to pray may enter". The Eucharist is frequently celebrated in this chapel, with

*Monument
to Countess Matilda di Canossa*

the inscription are by Andrea Bolgi (on the right) and Luigi Bernini, the brother of Gian Lorenzo (on the left).

On the right is the Baroque *funeral Monument of Innocent XII* [**21**] made by F. Della Valle and F. Fuga in 1746. The Pontiff (1691-1700) is seated while he gives his blessing. Next to the tomb are the allegorical figures of *Charity* and *Justice*.

Monument to Innocent XII

Chapel of the Blessed Sacrament, detail: the Tabernacle

hymns and community prayers. In bygone ages, the faithful would pause in silent prayer and contemplation of Jesus, the living bread come down from heaven. This bread is the Body of the Lord for the life of the world. Whoever eats this bread will have eternal life. The decision to reserve this chapel for the Blessed Sacrament implied the greatest commitment to its decoration. This is why the faithful who admire its beauty and harmony feel encouraged to pray and to reflect here. The most precious work is the *Tabernacle* of gilded bronze,

designed by Gian Lorenzo Bernini (1674) on the lines of the famous *tempietto* of St. Pietro in Montorio, the work of Bramante. Its charm is enhanced by statuettes of the twelve Apostles on the cornice and of Jesus on the miniature dome. It is encrusted with deep blue lapis lazuli which stands out against the golden background and is flanked by two of the loveliest angels in gilded bronze, kneeling in reverent prayer. Behind the altar is an altarpiece painted in oils by Pietro da Cortona (1596-1669) which celebrates the *Trinity*, God the Father,

the Son made man who died for us, the Holy Spirit who guides the Church. It is the only canvas in the whole basilica. The *Apocalypse aflame* and the *Saints in adoration* decorate the ceiling. In the spandrels are episodes from the Old Testament, prefiguring the Eucharist. The Eucharist is also the theme of the scenes in the lunettes. The mosaic covering the wall on the right was inspired by the *Ecstasy of St. Francis* by Domenichino.

Continuing along the aisle we encounter another two funeral monuments. On the left, the *monument of Gregory XIV* [**23**] (1590-1591) by Prospero of Brescia, with two statues representing *Religion* and *Justice*.

On the right is the *monument to Gregory XIII* (1572-1585), [**24**] who gave his name to the Gregorian University and the Gregorian calendar. Indeed, beneath the white marble figure of the Pope imparting a blessing, the work of Camillo Rusconi (1658-1728), is a bas-relief commemorating the *Reform of the calendar* desired by the Pontiff who decreed in 1582 that the days from 4 to 15 October be omitted, in order to gain 10 days with respect to the calendar then in use, which had been introduced by Julius Caesar. The statue is flanked by two allegorical figures: *Religion* and *Fortitude*.

At the intersection with the transept is the *Gregorian Chapel* [**25**], which is

Altar of Our Lady of Succor

named after Gregory VIII (1572-1585), the Pontiff who commissioned Giacomo Della Porta (1540-1602) to complete this work which had been begun by Michelangelo and continued by Barozzi and Vignola. It has been described as "the most beautiful chapel in the world" because of all its marbles, mother-of-pearl, precious stones, gilded bronze, multi-colored mosaics and stucco ornamentation. Its dome is 42 m. high.

On the back wall is the *Altar of Our Lady of Succor* [26], embellished with the rarest alabaster, amethysts and other semi-precious stones, and four superb columns of African marble and green porphyry, the work of G. Muziano (1528-1592). It is called after the 12th-century fresco framed above the altar, brought here by Gregory XIII in 1578. The remains of St. Gregory of Nazianzus (d. 390), one of the great theologians from Cappadocia, are preserved in a porphyry urn beneath the

Altar of St. Jerome

Altar of St. Basil the Great

altar. He is shown in the spandrels, together with St. Gregory the Great, St. Basil the Great and St. Jerome.

The chapel is adorned with splendid mosaics made mainly by Marcello Provenzale after designs by Girolamo Muziano, and by Salvatore Monosilio after designs by Nicola La Piccola. In the lunettes are *the Annunciation* and the Prophets *Isaiah* and *Ezekiel;* in the pendentives are the Latin Doctors *St. Jerome* and *St. Gregory the Great,* and the Greek Fathers, *St. Basil* and *St. Gregory of Nazianzus.*

On the right of the chapel is the *monument to Gregory XVI* [**27**] (1831-1846). The Neoclassical monument, made by Luigi Amici (1817-1897), shows the Pontiff seated on a throne, in the act of giving his blessing. The bas-relief on the urn portrays the *Institution of the Missions* by the Pontiff. The two allegorical lateral figures represent *Wisdom* and *Prudence.*

Returning to the aisle, against the pier supporting the dome we find *the Altar of St. Jerome* [**28**] decorated with a mosaic reproduction of Domenichino's famous painting (1614) of the *Last communion of St. Jerome.* Next to the 93-year old saint, St. Paul can be seen bending to kiss his hand; and a lion, its paws tucked under it, looks almost as if it were participating in his deep sorrow (the original canvas is in the Vatican Picture Gallery). At this point we note that most of the pictures in the basilica are mosaics, many of which are the work of P. Cristofari (whose preparatory cartoons can be found in various museums and churches).

On the other side of the pilaster, on the left of the aisle is the *Altar of St. Basil the Great* [**29**]. Pietro Subleyras (1699-1749) showed St. Basil celebrating solemn Mass for Epiphany in 372 and so involved in his devotion that he is oblivious to the entry of the Emperor Valentius with his retinue.

Opposite, on the right, is the *monument to Benedict XIV Lambertini* [**30**], a marble sculpture by Pietro Bracci (1700-1773).

The Pontiff is shown standing, in the act of blessing the Catholic world in the Jubilee of 1750. The allegorical figures below represent *Wisdom* (by Bracci) and *Impartiality* (by Gaspar Sibilia).

The right transept

We have now reached the transept of Sts. Processus and Martinian, the shortest bar of the Latin cross which corresponds to the northern bar of Michelangelo's original Greek cross. The vault in travertine was decorated in the 18th century by Vanvitelli with white and gold stucco ornaments. This right transept [**31**] was assigned as a hall for the sessions of the 700 Council Fathers who took part in the First Vatican Council here, opened by Pius IX on 8 December 1869 and suddenly interrupted on 18 July 1870 when Rome was taken by the Italian army.

The *central altar* is called after *Sts. Processus and Martinian* [**33**]. The mosaic altarpiece, after Jehan de Boulogne (Giambologna) (1594-1632) portrays the martyrdom of the two saints jailed in the Mamertine Prison, converted and baptized by St. Peter. The two columns in *giallo antico* marble which flank the altar, are valuable and rare.

The altar on the right is dedicated to St. Wenceslas [**32**], King of Bohemia. The mosaic showing the saint's martyrdom was inspired by a 1630 drawing by Angelo Caroselli. Beside the altar are two *oval* portraits in mosaic of *Sts. Cyril and Methodius,* patrons of Europe. *The*

altar on the left [**34**] is dedicated to St. Erasmus of Formia, Bishop and Martyr.

The mosaic is a reproduction of a painting by Nicholas Poussin (1594-1665), made by Cristofari in 1743.

A series of niches along the walls of the transept from the central nave contain statues of the holy founders of religious orders. In this right hand section of the transept we have: St. Gaetano Thiene, St. Jerome Emiliani, St. Joan Antide Thouret, St. Bruno, St. Paul of the Cross, St. Joseph Calasanctius, St. Bonfiglio, St. Frances Cabrini. Above the statues, in huge letters on a gold background on the frieze are the words: "O Petere, dixisti: Tu es Christus, filius Dei vivi. Ait Iesus: Beatus es Simon Bar Iona: quia caro, et sanguis non revelavit tibi" ("You are the Messiah', Simon Peter answered, the Son of the living God!' Jesus replied, Blessed are you, Simon son of Jonah! No mere man has revealed this to you, but my heavenly Father'") (Mt 16:16-17).

The passage between the right transept and the apse

Leaving the transept and continuing down the right aisle, on the left, next to the second pier supporting the dome, we find the *Altar of the Navicella* [**35**] whose name derives from the Gospel narrative of Jesus walking on the water. This mosaic was made in 1727 after a painting by Giovanni Lanfranco (1582-1647).

Opposite, on the right, is another artistic masterpiece: the *monument to Clement XIII* [**36**] (1758-1709) sculpted by Antonio Canova (1757-1822). It was the basilica's first monument in Neo-classical style.

It is dominated by the figure of the elderly Pope, clad in his papal robes and kneeling in prayer at the tomb.

On the left stands the noble, solemn statue of *Religion,* one of whose hands rests on the sarcophagus; the other holds the cross, the instrument of our salvation. On the right, the statue of the *Genius of death,* is calmly and languidly extinguishing the torch of life.

The sarcophagus is decorated with delicate reliefs of the figures of *Charity* and *Hope.*

On the wide plinth of the base, two splendid, crouching lions guard the tomb.

They are carved in travertine, while the rest of the monument is of white Carrara marble.

Continuing, we enter the *Chapel of St. Michael* at the end of the left aisle. The vault is decorated with the *Gloria of the Saints.* In the spandrels of the dome the *Doctors and Fathers of the*

Altar of the Navicella

Greek and Latin Churches are portrayed: *St. Leo the Great, St. Bernard of Clairvaux, St. Denys the Arcopagite, St. Gregory the Wonderworker.* In the lunettes: *Elias and the angel, Tobias and the Archangel Raphael, St. Peter baptizing St. Petronilla, St. Nicodemus giving communion to St. Petronilla.*

The altar on the right is dedicated to *St. Michael Archangel* [**37**]. The great altarpiece in a gilded bronze frame, is a 1757 mosaic reproduction of a painting of *St. Michael* by Guido Reni (1575-1642), a famous artist of the Bologna School.

The altar at the back is dedicated to *St. Petronilla* [**38**]. On it can be admired a scene of the *Burial of St. Petronilla, who is received into heaven by the heavenly Bridegroom,* one of the loveliest mosaics in the basilica. It is by Pier Paolo Cristofari after a painting by Giovanni Francesco Barbieri, known as Il Guercino (1590-1666). Under this altar

Altar of St. Michael Archangel

Altar of St. Petronilla

Monument to Clement X

are the relics of St. Petronilla, whose body, buried in the cemetery of Domitilla, was exhumed in 750 and venerated in a small shrine which Pépin le Bref had requested from the Pope and was therefore known as the "Rotonda of St. Petronilla".

When the saint's body was translated to St. Peter's basilica in 1606, it was this little chapel that became the national Church of France. Here, on May 31, the French community gathers solemnly to venerate the saint.

Between this chapel and the apse where part of the basilica's organ is displayed, on the right we find the *monument to Clement X* [**39**], designed by Mattia de Rossi (1637-1695), for which rare and precious marbles were used. The statue by Ercole Ferrata (d. 1686) shows the Pontiff enthroned. Beside him stand two allegorical figures, *Clemency* and *Beneficence*. Leonardo Leti's relief on the pedestal shows the *Opening of the Holy Door for the Jubilee of 1675.*

Opposite, on the left, is the *Altar of St. Peter raising Tabitha* [**40**], the woman of Jaffa (Acts 9:36-42). The miracle is shown in a mosaic inspired by a painting by Placido Costanzi (1702-1759).

Altar of St. Peter restoring Tabitha to life

The apse and the Altar of the Chair

The apse [41] is at the end of the central nave. In the center is the *Altar of the Chair of Peter* [42] a masterpiece which is unmistakably the work of Gian Lorenzo Bernini (1598-1659).

Every year on February 22, the Church celebrates the feast of the Chair of St. Peter, to commemorate St. Peter's teaching in Rome. Already in the second half of the 18th century an ancient wooden chair inlaid with ivory was venerated and traditionally held to be the episcopal chair on which St. Peter sat as he instructed the faithful of Rome. In fact, it is a throne in which fragments of acacia wood are visible, which could be part of the chair of St. Peter, encased in oak and reinforced with iron bands. Several rings facilitated its transportation during processions. Pope Alexander VII commissioned Bernini to build a sumptuous monument which would give prominence to this ancient wooden chair. Bernini built a throne in gilded bronze, richly ornamented with bas-reliefs in which the chair was enclosed: two pieces of furniture, one within the other.

On January 17, 1666 it was solemnly set above the altar.

The base of the altar is made of black and white marble from Aquitaine and red jasper from Sicily. Four gigantic statues (about 5 m. tall) in gilded bronze surround the Chair which looks almost as if it were suspended amidst the clouds. The two outer statues are figures of two Doctors of the Latin Church: *St. Ambrose* and *St. Agustine;* the two inner statues, with bare heads, are of two Doctors of the Greek Church: *St. Athanasius* and *St. John Chrysostom.* These saints represent the catholicity of the Church and at the same time, the consistency of the theologians' teaching with the doctrine of the Apostles.

Above the Chair are two angels bearing the tiara and keys, symbols of the Roman pontiff's authority.

On the Chair, are three bas-reliefs picked out in gold, which refer to the same number of Gospel episodes: the *Consignment of the keys, Feed my sheep,* and the *Washing of the feet.*

The whole composition is crowned by the fantastic gilt and stucco gloria peopled by a host of angels among rays of light and gigantic billowing clouds. In their midst is the precious window of Bohemian glass, divided into twelve sections as a tribute to the Twelve Apostles; a brilliant dove stands out against it, the symbol of the Holy Spirit, the soul of the Church which he never ceases to help and to guide.

Vanvitelli decorated the vault with gilded stucco. In the three medallions are portrayed: the *Consignment of the Keys,* the *Crucifixion of St. Peter* and the *Beheading of St. Paul.*

To the right of the Altar of the Chair is the *Monument to Urban VIII* [43] (1623-1644), designed by Bernini in 1627 and completed in 1646, after he had worked on it for 20 years. The artist wished to offer his very best to this Pope who had discovered him and entrusted him with such important projects. The Pontiff is shown in the act of giving his blessing, solemnly dressed in his papal robes. The statue is not made of marble but of bronze with gold highlights. Above the *sarcophagus,* in Portoro marble, is a skeleton of *Death,* in the act of writing the Pope's name on a scroll of parchment which it is clasping. Beside it, in

Altar of the Chair, detail

white Carrara marble, the beautiful allegorical figures of *Justice*, who is raising her eyes almost as if to trust herself
to divine justice, and *Charity*, who holds
a child in her arms and looks sorrowfully
at another, pointing to the dead Pope.
Even the bees of the Barberini Pope's
coat of arms, which we have already
seen on the altar of the Confession, seem
to have lost their sense of direction. On
this monument too, we admire the bal-
ance between architecture and sculpture, a great merit of Bernini's style.
Typical of this monument is the use,
mentioned above, which has been made
of various types of material.

On the left of the Altar of the Chair is
the *Monument to Paul III* (1534-
1549) [**44**], the Pope who in 1545
convoked the Council of Trent and in
1547 commissioned Michelangelo to
direct the work of building the basilica.
The monument was made by Giacomo
della Porta (1533-1602) who probably
used a drawing by Michangelo. The
bronze *statue of the Pope* crowns the
pyramidal monument. Below, two
marble figures allude to *Justice* and
Prudence.

The first statue is a likeness of the
Pope's sister, Julia; the second, of the
Pope's mother.

This monument was first placed in the Gregorian Chapel, then in 1628 Bernini moved it here.

In the tribune of the Chair, a continuation of the central nave and the transept, are niches with statues representing the holy founders of religious orders.

Here on the right are: *St. Elias, St. Francis de Sales, St. Dominic, St. Francesco Caracciolo;* on the left: *St. Benedict, St. Frances of Rome, St. Francis of Assisi, St. Alphonsus of Liguori.*

Four great tablets beneath the statues recall the proclamation of the dogma of the Immaculate Conception by Pius IX on December 8, 1854.

Above, on the golden background of the frieze, is the Latin inscription: "O Pastor Ecclesiae, tu omnes Christi pascis agnos et oves" (O pastor of the Church, you feed all Christ's lambs and sheep).

On the right is the same writing in Greek:

"Σὺ βόσκεισ τὰ αρνία, συ ποίμαινεισ τὰ προβάτια Χριστὸι".

The passage between the apse and the left transept

We now begin our visit of the left side of the basilica, in the opposite direction from the itinerary we took for the right side; we start from the apse and proceed towards the entrance. Leaving the apse, in the passage from the left aisle where the keyboard and part of the basilica's great organ stands, on the right is the *monument to Alexander VIII* (1689-1691)

[45], after a design by Arrigo di San Martino (d. 1726). The bronze statue by Giuseppe Bertoni represents the Pope; the two majestic statues in marble by Angelo Rossi, are *Religion and Prudence*. The marble bas-relief in the center below, also by Rossi, portrays the *Canonization* by Alexander VIII in 1690, of *St. Laurence Giustiniani, St. John of Capestrano, St. John of San Facondo, St. Paschal Baylon, St. John of God*. This monument is a typical example of the use of various types of marble and stones, alabaster, breccia, *giallo antico*.

Part of the great organ of the basilica

Opposite, against the pilaster, is the *Altar of St. Peter healing the cripple* [46]. The altarpiece, a mosaic reproduction of the original by Francesco Mancini (1679-1758), shows St. Peter healing the cripple in Jerusalem by the temple gate called "the Beautiful" (Acts 3:1-10).

We now enter the *Chapel of Our Lady of the Column* [47], surmounted by one of the smaller cupolas, a corner chapel, located at the end of the left aisle.

On the right of the chapel is the *Altar of St. Leo the Great* [48] (440-461), the first pope to be buried in the basilica. When he died, he was buried in the sacristy of the ancient basilica, and his body was subsequently moved to the *Porticus Pontificum*. Finally, Paul V desired it to be translated to this chapel, together with the remains of Popes Leo II, Leo III, Leo IV and Gregory XIII. The great carved marble altarpiece by Alessandro Algardi (1602-1625) portrays the *Meeting of Pope Leo the Great with Attila*, King of the Huns, whose advance on Rome in 452 the Pope had succeeded in halting, thereby saving Rome from destruction.

On the left is the *Altar of Our Lady of the Column* [49] called after the image of the Blessed Virgin painted on a column from the old basilica.

In 1607 it was placed on this altar designed by Giacomo Della Porta, framed by the finest marbles and precious alabaster columns.

After the Second Vatican Council, Paul VI honored it with the title of "Mater Ecclesiae". In 1981 John Paul II had a mosaic reproduction of it set on the external wall of the *palazzo* facing St. Peter's Square, where it can also be seen illuminated at night.

This chapel is covered by one of the basilica's minor cupolas which lets in light that enhances the colors of the altar.

On the vault of the dome are portraits of the Litany of Loreto; in the spandrels: *St. Bonadventure, St. Thomas Aquinas, St. Cyril of Alexandria, St. John Damascene.*

In the lunettes are portrayed: *The Virgin Mother and Child, the Dream of St. Joseph, and the Kings, David and Solomon.*

In the passage between this chapel and the transept, on the left against the pilaster supporting the cupola is the *Altar of the Sacred Heart* [50], which on the occasion of St. Margaret Mary Alacoque's canonization in 1923, was decorated with a mosaic inspired by a painting by Carlo Muccioli (1857-1933).

Opposite and on the right, is the famous funeral monument of Alexander VII (1655-1667) [51], the last great masterpiece of the 80-year old Bernini who was assisted by various artists. The Pontiff, kneeling and absorbed in prayer, is not disturbed by the sudden appearance of *Death*, who, raising a heavy pall, brandishes an hour-glass to indicate that time has passed. The four statues represent the virtues practiced by the Pontiff: in the foreground is *Charity* by G. Mazzuoli, with a child in her arms, and *Truth*, by Morelli and Cartari, who sets a foot on a map of the world, and precisely on England where the Pope sought in vain to quell the growth of Anglicanism; on the second level is *Prudence*, by G. Cartari, and *Justice*, by L. Balestri.

The skeleton of Death is in gilded bronze; the splendid drapery which conceals part of the door under it is made of Sicilian jasper; the statues are carved in white marble and the plinth in black, as a sign of mourning.

Altar of St. Leo the Great

Altar of Our Lady of the Column

Altar of the Sacred Heart

Monument to Alexander VII

The left transept or St. Joseph's Cross

The left transept [**52**] resembles a chapel, open to all, but reserved for recollection and prayer. On weekdays, the basilica's scheduled Masses are celebrated at the main altar, dedicated to St. Joseph, at 10, 11 and 12. On Sundays, only one Mass is celebrated at 13.00. Communion is also distributed here to the faithful who ask for it. The Blessed Sacrament, a memorial of Christ's love for us until the end of time, is constantly preserved in the Tabernacle. All the faithful who enter the basilica pass here and genuflect before the Blessed Sacrament, pausing a few moments, kneeling or sitting in the pews, to pray.

There are three altars. The *Central Altar* [**54**] was previously dedicated to the *Holy Apostles, Simon and Jude, and Thaddeus*, whose relics are preserved in an ancient sarcophagus. John XXIII dedicated it to *St. Joseph*, Mary's husband and the putative father of Jesus. The mosaic which now decorates the altar was designed by A. Funi (1890-1972), and shows St. Joseph. Flanking the altar are two oval mosaic portraits of the two Apostles, after paintings by Vincent Camuccini.

On the right is the *Altar of St. Thomas* [**53**] above which is a mosaic altarpiece inspired by a painting of the *Disbelief of the Apostle Thomas*, by Vincenzo Camuccini (1771-1844). The relics of Pope St. Boniface IV who consecrated the Pantheon for Christian worship are kept beneath the altar.

On the left is the *Altar of the Cru-cifixion of St. Peter,* [**55**] with a mosaic reproduction of a picture by Guido Reni (1575-1642) showing St. Peter crucified upside down. An ancient tradition claims that St. Peter suffered martyrdom pre-cisely where the altar stands. In fact part of the basilica is actually built on the site of Nero's Circus.

The series of niches containing stat-ues of the holy founders of religious orders continues from the central nave along the walls of this part of the transept. Here we have: *St. John of God, St. Mary Euphrasia Pellettier, St. Peter Nolasco, St. Juliana Falconieri, St. Louise de Marillac, St. Angela Merici, St. Norbert, St. William.* Above, against a golden background on the trabeation the inscription reads: "Dicit ter tibi, Petre, Iesus: Diligis me? Cui ter, o electe, respondens ais: O Domine, tu omnia nosti, tu scis quia amo te" ("A third time, Jesus asked him, 'Simon, son of John, do you love me?' 'Yes, Lord', Peter said, 'You know that I love you'") (Jn 21:17).

The left aisle

Passing from the transept to the left aisle, on the left is the *Altar of Ananias and Sapphira* [**56**] or Altar of the Lie. The mosaic is after a painting by Cristo-foro Roncalli, known as Pomarancio (1552-1626), and shows the punishment of the couple who had lied to St. Peter.

Opposite, on the right [**57**], is the *Monument to Pius VIII* (1829-1830), by Pietro Tenerani (1789-1869), in the Neoclassical style. The Pontiff is kneel-ing; above him is the statue of *Christ enthroned,* and below, are the *statues*

Altar of St. Thomas

Altar of the Lie

Monument to Pius VIII and the entrance to the Sacristy and the Treasury of St. Peter's

of *Sts. Peter and Paul*. On the base are the allegorical figures of *Prudence* and *Justice*.

Under this monument a door leads to the *Sacristy* and the *Treasury*.

On the right is the *Clementine Chapel* [58] commissioned by Pope Clement VIII (1592-1605), whose coat of arms stands out against the paving. It was begun by Michelangelo and completed by Giacomo Della Porta (1540-1602) for the Jubilee in 1600. The *altar* [59] is dedicated to *St. Gregory the Great* (590-604). In a sarcophagus beneath the altar his remains are preserved, brought here in 1606. This Pope, also called the "Savior of the Church" and the "Defender of Rome", is associated with the name of the Gregorian chant or plainsong which he promoted.

He was also responsible for the evangelization of England. The splendid mosaic on the altarpiece, after a picture painted in 1625 by Andrea Sacchi (15991661), is the work of Alessandro Cocchi and Vincenzo Castellini, and portrays the saint as he shows the faithful cloth stained by the blood which miraculously flowed from the relics of some martyrs.

In the spandrels of the dome are four great saints, Doctors of the Church: *Ambrose* and *Augustine*, of the Latin Church, *John Chrysostom* and *Athanasius*, of the Greek Church.

In the lunettes: *The Visitation*, *St. Zachary and St. Elizabeth*, *Malachi the angel* and *Daniel in the lions' den*. The designs are by Cristoforo Roncalli, known as Pomarancio; the mosaics are the work of Marcello Provenzale and Paolo Rossetti.

The *Monument of Pius VII* (1800-1823) [60] occupies part of the left wall of the Clementine Chapel. He was the Pope imprisoned by Napoleon and exiled to Fontainebleau. After his liberation, he did all he could for the emperor exiled at Sant'Elena and helped his elderly mother. The weary Pontiff is seated majestically on his throne and is blessing all, friends and enemies. The monument is the work of the Danish sculptor, Bertel Thorvaldsen (1770-1844), Roman by adoption. Beside the Pontiff are two allegorical figures: the *Genius of time* and *History*, intent on recording the Pope's achievements with the hourglass and a book; on the pedestal are another two statues which represent *Fortitude*, with the lionskin, and *Wisdom*, with the book and the owl.

Returning to the aisle, against the pier supporting the dome is the *Altar of the Transfiguration* [61], with a mosaic reproduction of one of the masterpieces of Raphael (1483-1520), the great painter's last work. Jesus, bathed in light, is borne aloft between Moses and Elijah, also in ecstasy, while the Apostles Peter, James and John, prostrate, contemplate this glimpse of paradise. On the left, almost hidden, are Sts. Felicissimus and Agapitus, who are commemorated on 6 August, the Feast of the Transfiguration.

In the lower part, the healing of the young man who was "possessed" is portrayed, giving the scene a sense of agitation, while in the upper part of the picture, profound peace is contemplated. In the center, a kneeling woman represents the Church which brings peace and hope and invites us to await them as gifts from above.

In the passage way are two monuments. On the right, the white marble *Monument to Leo XI* [62] by Alessandro Algardi (1595-1654). The Pontiff is seated in the center. The roses carved on the plinth and the inscription "Sic florui", refer to the fact that he reigned only 27 days, in 1605. Beside him are two female figures: *Majesty* and *Gen-*

Altar of St. Gregory the Great

erosity. On the sacrophagus, are scenes of the abjuration of Protestantism made by Henry IV of France when Leo was still a cardinal and apostolic nuncio, and the signing of the peace treaty between Spain and France.

On the left, towards the central nave, is the funeral *Monument of Innocent XI* [**63**] (1676-1689), the work of the French sculptor Pierre Etienne Monnot. The Pontiff, making a solemn, oratorial gesture, is seated on the throne set above a sarcophagus, in *giallo antico*

marble, flanked by *Religion* and *Justice.* A bas-relief on the urn by John Sobieski, shows the *Victory over the Turks in Vienna* in 1683.

At this point we have reached the section of the basilica with the three aisles built by Carlo Maderno between 1606 and 1614.

A little further, on the right of the aisle is the *Chapel of the Choir* [**64**]. Its design was traditionally attributed to Giacomo della Porta (1540-1602), but today it is thought to be the work of Carlo

Altar of the Transfiguration

Maderno. It owes its name to the fact that the canons of the basilica used to celebrate the Liturgy of the Hours here as a choir. The gate of the chapel, usually closed, is of exquisite workmanship.

The *altarpiece* [**65**], by Pietro Bianchi (1694-1740), shows the *Virgin Immaculate* in glory surrounded by angels and venerated by *Sts. Francis of Assisi, Anthony of Padua, John Chrysostom*. On December 8,1854, on the occasion of the proclamation of the Dogma of the Immaculate Conception, Pius IX crowned the image of Mary. To mark the 50th anniversary of the Dogma, St. Pius X added a second crown, consisting of twelve stars, gleaming with twelve brilliants, donated by various nations.

Beneath the altar are the remains of St. John Chrysostom and relics of St. Francis and St. Antony. The paschal candle stands on a black and white marble column with a porphyry base, in accordance with Paul VI's wishes.

The vault of the chapel, divided by four Corinthian pilasters, is decorated

with fine gilded stucco ornaments on a white background, showing the *Creation*, the *Crossing of the Red Sea*, the *Baptism of Jesus*. In the dome are the *Vision of the angels* and *the Elect* of the Apocalypse. In the vault are shown: *Habakuk and the angel*, *Daniel in the lions' den*, *David*, *Jonah inside the whale*. In the lunettes, *Deborah and Barak*, *Judith with Holofern's head*, *Moses and Aaron*, *Ozaziah* and *Uzziah* and *Jeremiah*.

The dark wooden choir against the walls has a triple row of stalls, adorned with magnificent bas-reliefs and decorations; above it on each side are two historical organs.

Between this chapel and the next is the *Monument to St. Pius X (1904-1914)*, [**66**] planned by the architect Florestano Di Fausto and carved by the sculptor Pietro Astorri in 1923. The Pontiff, carved from the whitest marble, is shown standing, his arms outstretched to the faithful. Around the door and on its panels are the most beautiful bas-reliefs in bronze illuminated with gold, recalling episodes from the saint's life.

On the left is the funeral *Monument of Innocent VIII* (1484-1492) [**67**], a very fine work made between 1493 and 1498 by Antonio del Pollaiolo (1431 1408), which was formerly in the old St. Peter's. The Pontiff sits solemn and authoritative on his throne. He is imparting a blessing with his right hand, while with his left, he shows the lance that pierced Jesus' side. The relic of the lance which was presented to him by the Sultan Bajazet II, is now kept, as we have seen, close to the Altar of the *Confessio*. Next to the Pontiff are the four cardinal virtues: *Prudence*, *Justice*, *Fortitude* and *Tem-*

Altar of Mary Immaculate

Chapel of the Presentation of the Virgin Mary at the Temple

perance. The upper lunette displays the three theological virtues: *Faith, Hope* and *Charity.* In the lower section of the monument, the Pontiff is shown lying in a sarcophagus, shrouded in the stillness of death.

Then on the right is the *Chapel of the Presentation* [**69**], named after the

mosaic retablero over the main altar from a painting by Giovanni Francesco Romanelli (1610-1662) of the *Presentation of the Virgin.* In the gilded bronze and crystal casket beneath the altar is the body of St. Pius X (1904-1914), clad in solemn papal robes.

The chapel is decorated with mosaics

*Monument
to Benedict XV*

by Carlo Maratta (1625-1713). In the pendentives of the dome: *Aaron with the thurible, Noah and the ark, Gideon amd the fleece, Balaam and the Star of Jacob.* In the lunettes: *Moses removes his sandals before the burning bush, Miriam and the Red Sea crossing, Judith and Holofernes, Jael and Sisera, Joshua makes the sun stand still, Isaiah and the cloud.* The vault is decorated with scenes of the *Coronation of the Virgin* and *Lucifer's defeat.*

Against the wall on the right is a bronze *Monument to Pope John XXIII* (1958-1963) [**68**]. On the left we can see the *Monument to Benedict XV*

(1914-1922) [**70**], made in 1928 by the sculptor Pietro Canonica (1869-1959). The Pontiff is absorbed in prayer, kneeling on a tomb which commemorates the First World War which he described as a "useless massacre". The tomb is covered in olive branches, symbols of peace. Above the statue is Mary, presenting Jesus, Prince of Peace, to the world in flames.

Under the next arch on the right is the *monument to Maria Clementina Sobieska,* (1702-1735) [**71**], niece of

King John II of Poland, who in 1719 married the Pretender to the throne of England, James III Stuart. The princess is portrayed in a medallion held up by a cherub and by the statue representing *Charity,* the work of Pietro Bracci (1700-1773).

Under the monument is the exit from the dome.

Opposite, toward the central nave is the impressive *Monument to the Stuarts* [**72**], a masterpiece by Antonio Canova (1757-1822), who completed it in 1819,

commissioned by of the British Government. It celebrates James III (1688-1766), Pretender to the Kingdom of England, the husband of Maria Clementina Sobieska, and their two sons, Charles (1720-1788) the Duke, and Henry (1725-1807), Cardinal of York and Bishop of Frascati, Ostia and Velletri. All three died in Rome, where they had been exiled. In the center of the white marble stele an inscription recalls these last three members of the Stuart family. On it are portrait busts of them in profile. Above, is the escutcheon of the Stuarts with two lions rampant. Below, next to a closed door, are two of the loveliest sorrowful angels, their wings folded and their heads inclined over two upside-down torches which they are about to extinguish. Above the door a biblical sentence encourages Christian hope: "Blessed are those who die in the Lord".

George III of England covered the expenses of this monument, begun in 1817 and completed in 1821.

The Chapel of the Baptistery, detail of the baptismal font

Thus we reach the last chapel in the left aisle. It is the *Chapel of the Baptistery* [**73**], one of the basilica's most beautiful chapels and built after a design by Carlo Fontana (1634-1714). In the center is the *baptismal font*, still used on Sundays to administer the sacrament of baptism.

The original 5th-century font, which dates back to Pope Damasus, was replaced by a sarcophagus used as a font, and then in the 17th century by the present-day font whose red porphyry basin was made from an ornament on an ancient pagan sepulcher, later used to cover the sarcophagus of Otto II who died in 983. The Rococo cover in gilded bronze with volutes and cherubs, dominated by *the Lamb of God,* is the work of Giovanni Giardoni.

In the forepart, two bronze angels bear a relief of the Most Holy Trinity

Chapel of the Baptistery

and a geographical representation of Italy.

The altarpiece in mosaic was made in 1722, reproducing a design by the painter from the Marches, Carlo Maratta, which dates to 1696-1698. It represents the *Baptism of Jesus* by John the Baptist, in the River Jordan.

Beside the chapel are another two mosaics: on the right, *St. Peter baptizing the Centurion Cornelius* inspired by a painting by Andrea Procaccini, executed in 1711; and on the left, *St. Peter baptizing Sts. Processus and Martinian,* his two fellow-prisoners, after a painting by Giuseppe Passeri.

The dome is decorated with mosaics, from originals by Francesco Trevisani da Capodistria. In the spandrels are portrayed the races of the four continents which became Christian: *Europe, Asia, Africa, America.* In the lunettes are various *baptismal scenes: Jesus baptizes Peter, St. Peter baptizes the Centurion Cornelius, St. Philip baptizes the Eunuch of Queen Candace, St. Silvester*

Tablet with a list of the popes buried in St. Peter's

baptizes Constantine, and several symbols of baptism: *Moses causes the water to spring from the rock, Noah prays before the rainbow of the Covenant.*

In this chapel, on October 16, 1994, Pope John Paul II's new coat of arms was set into the marble pavement in the center of the chapel. Against the lapis lazuli background of the escutcheon, the bars of the cross and the letter "M" (for Maria) stand out clearly in *giallo antico.*

The keys, miter and *infulae* stand out against the black French marble. The letters of the motto: "Totus tuus", in *giallo antico* are inlaid in green ser-

Interior of the sacristy

pentine which borders the black background at both sides.

At the end of the aisle is the Door of Death.

The Sacristy and Treasury of St. Peter's

In the left aisle, under the monument of Pius VIII, is the entrance to the sacristy. It is a building which was attached to the basilica under Pius VI who commissioned Carlo Marchionni (1702-1786) to build it in 1776. On the right of the entrance, is a list of the popes buried in St. Peter's and a statue of St. Andrew in polychrome marble, and then a gallery, decorated with columns of the rarest marbles and bronze busts of Benedict XIII and Paul IV. Finally, there is an imposing statue of Pius VI by Agostino Penna. The *main Sacristy*, which is octagonal, is decorated with

The papal tiara with which the bronze statue of St. Peter is crowned on June 29

eight columns from Hadrian's Villa in Tivoli.

From the sacristy, the ten rooms which house the *Treasury* can be visited. Worthy of note are: *the fourth-century twisted marble column*, decorated with vine tendrils; the *gilded-metal cock*, which formerly adorned the bell tower of the old St. Peter's; the *Chair of St. Peter*, a copy of the oak throne which Charles the Bald presented to Pope John VIII in 875; the *Dalmatic*, said to have belonged to Charlemagne, but which is in fact an 11th-century Byzantine masterpiece;

9th-century bronze cock

The central dome and the ten minor cupolas of the basilica

the red *cope* and the *tiara* embellished with precious stones, which are put on the statue of St. Peter in the central nave for important solemnities, the *Stuart chalice*; the *Crux Vaticana*, made of leather studded with silver and precious stones and which contains fragments of the cross of Jesus; numerous *reliquaries and valuable candelabra*; a plaster cast of Michelangelo's *Pietà made in 1934-35*, thanks to which it was possible to restore the original perfectly after it was vandalized in 1972; the *funerary monument of Sixtus IV, founder of the Sistine Chapel and the Apostolic Library*, sculpted by Antonio del Pollaiolo. One of the most important sources of documentation of the art and faith of Christians in first-century Rome is the *Sarcophagus of Junio Bassus*, a noble and prefect of Rome, and a convert to Christianity. The marble sarcophagus, a

fourth century-work, is carved with reliefs showing scenes from the Old and New Testaments.

The ascent to the dome

The entrance to the dome is located in the courtyard on the right of the basilica. An elevator can be taken to the first level which gives access to the terrace over the central nave, over which tower the central dome, two large circular cupolas which are purely decorative since they are unrelated to the interior, four smaller circular cupolas which correspond to the four large chapels at the end of the transept, and six elliptical cupolas which give light to the side aisles. The rest of the ascent must be made on foot.

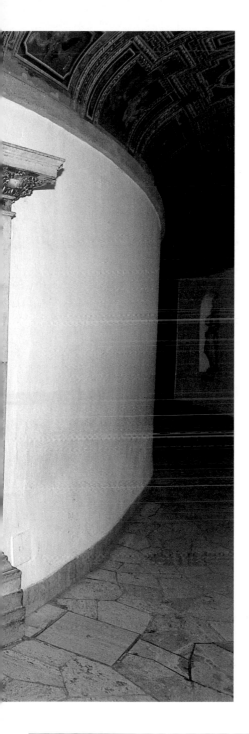

The Vatican Grottoes: the grill at the entrance to the Clementine Chapel, with the tomb of St Peter, seen from the side opposite that of the Niche of the Palliums (see p. 43).

From the gallery on the inside, the interior of the basilica can be admired and on the outside, one can view the magnificent panorama of Rome's churches, bell-towers and rooftops, with the Alban hills in the background.

The Vatican Grottoes

At the foot of the statues in each of the four central piers there are entrances which lead down stairs to the Vatican Grottoes (or crypt of the basilica). The usual entrance is the one in the pier of St. Longinus.

On entering the Grottoes, the visitor first sees vestiges of the basilica built by Constantine. In fact, the new basilica was built at a higher level than the old one, so that the foundations of the old basilica are now visible in the Grottoes.

Secondly, it is also possible to see the remains of a first-century Roman necropolis, where little by little Christian tombs were added to the pagan tombs. Archeological excavations in the last century led to important discoveries. Many rooms have therefore been built, in which, as well as the finds of the excavations, monuments, mosaics and sculptures from the old basilica are also displayed.

Lastly, along the walls and between the massive pillars that support the basilica, are the tombs of numerous Popes. The faithful pause to pray before them and often lay flowers on the tombs of the recent Pontiffs: Pius XII, John XXIII, Paul VI, John Paul I.

Monument to Pius VI, sculpted by Antonio Canova

Tomb of Pope Boniface VIII, in whose pontificate the celebration of the Jubilees began

Tomb of Pope John XXIII, who convoked the Second Vatican Council